THE GOD OF ALL COMFORT

This is the book that Kirsten gave me and I thought it so wonderful. But her book was smaller & thicker. This is the form this book is in now. I got it through Barnes & Noble.

THE GOD OF ALL COMFORT

HOPE FOR CHRISTIANS IN A WORLD OF SUFFERING

PHILLIP EICHMAN

Outskirts Press, Inc.
Denver, Colorado

The opinions expressed in this manuscript are solely the opinions of the author and do not represent the opinions or thoughts of the publisher. The author has represented and warranted full ownership and/or legal right to publish all the materials in this book.

The God of All Comfort
Hope for Christians in a World of Suffering
All Rights Reserved.
Copyright © 2010 Phillip Eichman
v2.0

Unless otherwise noted all Scripture quotations are taken from the New International Version, copyright 1973, 1978, and 1984 by the International Bible Society.

Quotations designated as "Phillips" are taken from *The New Testament in Modern English* by J. B. Phillips, copyright 1958, 1959, 1960 by J. B. Phillips, published by The Macmillan Company.

This book may not be reproduced, transmitted, or stored in whole or in part by any means, including graphic, electronic, or mechanical without the express written consent of the publisher except in the case of brief quotations embodied in critical articles and reviews.

Outskirts Press, Inc.
http://www.outskirtspress.com

ISBN: 978-1-4327-6549-1

Outskirts Press and the "OP" logo are trademarks belonging to Outskirts Press, Inc.

PRINTED IN THE UNITED STATES OF AMERICA

Contents

Preface vii
A World of Hurting 1
What Is Pain? 5
Pain and Suffering in the Bible 11
The Problem of Pain 15
Job and the Problem of Suffering 23
Suffering and God's Providence 29
The Christian and Suffering 35
Death: the Final Enemy 43
The Christian and Hope 53
Final Thoughts 59
Notes 61
Further Reading 65

Preface

This book represents a personal search for hope, assurance, and meaning in a world where we see so much pain and suffering. I have been working on this for a long time and even though I am still not completely satisfied with it, I sincerely hope that it will be an encouragement to others.

I would like to dedicate this to the memory of my parents. They are both gone from this world. Like others of God's people, however, they are now with the Lord and no longer need to be concerned with the matters discussed here. For them faith has become sight.

Phillip Eichman

A World of Hurting

Praise be to the God and Father of our Lord Jesus Christ, the Father of compassion and God of all comfort, who comforts us in all our troubles, so that we can comfort those in any trouble with the comfort we ourselves have received from God.

2 Corinthians 1:3-4

Things happen in our lives that often leave us hurting. It might be illness, the death of a loved one, loss of a job, financial problems, unfaithfulness of a mate, a child on drugs, or any number of physical, emotional, or even spiritual traumas that bring pain into our lives. These may leave us with feelings of fear, anxiety, helplessness, and even hopelessness and despair.

If by some chance we have escaped pain in our own lives, then we only need to look around us to see that we do live in a world of suffering. It isn't hard to find someone that is hurting. We need only to look in our neighborhood, at school, at work, at church, or watch the evening news. Pain and suffering are universal and have transcended not only time, but also all social, economic, and political boundaries. Wars, poverty, diseases, accidents, and natural disasters add to the toll. The magnitude of hurting, physically, as well as emotionally and spiritually, in our world is difficult to imagine.

Where does a person turn for strength during times of suffering? Many turn to something greater or higher than themselves--religion. Yet many religions are fatalistic. The Muslim, for example, will say, "It is the will of Allah." Most eastern religions either accept pain as some form of punishment or at best, the result of fate.

Even Judaism did not provide much help for the suffering. God, as perceived by the Jews, was stern and distant, and often punished people severely for disobedience. There is little in the Old Testament for one who is suffering. There are exceptions, primarily in the Psalms and prophetic books. Many of these are beautiful passages of hope and encouragement.

The greatest source of strength in suffering is to be found in Christianity. It is within the person of Jesus Christ and the pages of the New Testament that God has most completely revealed himself as a being of compassion and comfort for those living in a world of suffering.

Early in his ministry, Jesus visited the synagogue in Nazareth where he had grown up (Luke 4:16-21). He was invited to read from the Scriptures and chose a passage from the book of Isaiah (61:1-2). Luke, in his account gives a somewhat abbreviated version of the passage. In Isaiah we read the complete text:

The Spirit of the Sovereign Lord is on me, because the Lord has anointed me to preach good news to the poor. He has sent me to bind up the brokenhearted, to proclaim freedom for the captives and release from darkness for the prisoners, to proclaim the year of the Lord's favor and the day of vengeance of our God, to comfort all who mourn, and provide for those who grieve in Zion--to bestow on them a crown of beauty instead of ashes, the oil of gladness instead of mourning, and a garment of praise instead of a spirit of despair.

Although written centuries before, this passage certainly describes the ministry of Jesus. Not only did he bring the good news of salvation but also a ministry of healing. It was Jesus who was willing to reach out to touch the leper, to heal the woman of her bleeding disorder, and to raise his friend Lazarus from the dead.

We no longer have the power to touch and heal, as did Jesus and the apostles. The message of Christianity, however, is still one of healing, hope, and comfort. God is truly the God of all comfort and has not left us alone or without hope in our suffering.

Many people naively believe that God will somehow bless Christians with a life free of pain, anxiety, sorrow, or unhappiness. Christianity, however, is not a vaccine that will make a person immune to pain and suffering. We need only look to the examples of those who lived before us or to those living with us now to see that Christians also experience pain and suffering. Yet we need not despair, for just as in the days of Jesus and the apostles, there is good news for those who are in Christ. The message of

Christianity is one of hope. And, through the compassion and comfort of God and the power of the resurrection, Christians can overcome not only pain, suffering, and illness, but even death itself.

What Is Pain?

And a woman was there who had been subject to bleeding for twelve years. She had suffered a great deal under the care of many doctors and had spent all she had, yet instead of getting better she grew worse.

Mark 5:25-26

The title of the book, *Pain: The Gift Nobody Wants*, by Dr. Paul Brand and Philip Yancey, fairly well summarizes how we look at pain.[1] The word itself carries with it negative connotations. For most of us the experience of pain is something to be avoided if at all possible.

Albert Schweitzer wrote: "Pain is a more terrible lord of mankind than even death himself."[2] Schweitzer was writing primarily from his experiences as a physician in Africa among those who have little access to medical care. The thought, however, applies to all of us, even those who have access to the most modern medical advances. Most of us do fear pain, especially extreme or excruciating pain associated with serious injuries or illness such as cancer, even more than dying.

Pain is not, however, always a bad thing. Pain is a signal that lets us know when we have experienced an injury or that our body is fighting an infection. Pain is a natural response of the body and as essential as any other physiological process.

Physical Pain

I have known people who said, "I have never had a headache in my life." I have not been as fortunate myself and sometimes envy these people. Yet even someone who has never had a headache has probably experienced some type of pain. Pain is a natural process and a part of life.

It is interesting that the English word "pain" comes from a Latin word which means a fine or penalty. We recognize pain as being something unpleasant and generally think of it in negative terms.

Physical pain is a response of the nervous system to injury or disease. We can define it biologically in terms of sensory neurons and nerve impulses, but the bottom line is that pain hurts. A child falls down and scrapes her knee. She says, "Mommy, it hurts!" Or a person has the flu and says, "I hurt all over."

As much as we dislike it, however, pain is a necessary and essential part of life. A world without pain is certainly a pleasant thought but physical existence without pain would be impossible. Without the sensation of pain a person might suffer from a disease or injury without realizing it, possibly leading to something much more serious.

There are those individuals who have been born with a rare condition in which they have no sensation of pain. Burns, cuts, bruises, and even broken or dislocated limbs cause them no discomfort. At first this may seem like a blessing--a life free of pain. Such is not the case, however, because even the slightest injury or illness could pose a serious threat if left unnoticed or untreated.

Similar effects can be caused by certain diseases, such as leprosy, that can destroy the nerves and leave the victim with no feeling in larger areas of the body like hands, feet, or even an entire arm or leg. As a result, persons with leprosy can seriously injure themselves and not realize it. They might have a burn, cut, blister, or infected wound and not feel the body's warning signals.

Although physical pain is a normal physiological process, it is still unpleasant and is avoided by most normal humans and animals. Nevertheless, we all suffer pain to one degree or another. The most common type of pain is acute pain or short-term pain. This type of pain is caused typically by an injury or disease such as a sore throat, scraped knee, or sprained ankle.

Acute pain is a signal from the body to the brain indicating that some part of the body has been damaged by injury or illness. Acute pain may be very intense, but usually lasts for only a short period of time, ranging from a few minutes to a few days.

In contrast, chronic pain, or long-term pain, lasts for weeks, months, or even years. Such pain is associated with chronic or long-standing illnesses such as arthritis, cancer, or other long-term health problems. Chronic pain is much more difficult for the person to deal with. Chronic pain can wear the person down, not only physically but also emotionally and at times even spiritually. Chronic pain can even dominate a person's life and lead to other physical and emotional problems.

It is difficult to fully understand chronic pain unless a person has experienced it. Most people have never had pain that lasted for more than a few days, and even then they could look forward to "getting well again." Such is not the case with chronic pain; it is often something that a person can expect to experience for a long time and perhaps even the rest of his or her life.

Researchers have found that there are actually two types of pain receptors in the nervous system. One type responds primarily to acute pain and the sensation is sharp and intense. The other type responds to chronic pain and results in a dull ache or burning sensation. It is ironic that even within our nervous system there is a differentiation between types of physical pain.

Emotional Pain

Emotional pain is much more difficult to define or explain, but it is just as real as physical pain. The loss of a loved one, a divorce, an unfaithful mate, a child who has run away, or similar events can cause pain that hurts just as much as any physical illness or injury. Aspirin may temporarily relieve a headache, but emotional pain is often much more difficult to treat.

When I was younger, I felt that Christians have such a perfect state of mind that they should never have any anxiety, fear, depression, or any other cause of mental pain or anguish. I realize now that Christianity is perfect, but Christians are not. Christianity is the best possible way of living, but as pointed out earlier, it does not make one immune to pain or suffering.

Christians hurt just like everyone else. The difference is in their relationship with God. Christians have a special status. The death of Christ was the atoning sacrifice for sin. Thus, the Christian's sins have been blotted out by the blood of Jesus.

Guilt from past mistakes should no longer burden Christians for they are a redeemed and justified people. Further, God has promised to comfort us and to bless us beyond anything that we might imagine. Nowhere in Scripture did God promise to remove pain from our physical existence, but he did not leave us without hope.

Pain And Stress

Not only is pain caused by injury, illness, or emotional traumas, but also we now know that pain can also be brought on by stress. We all have a certain amount of stress in our lives. In fact a little stress is beneficial--it keeps us on our toes and keeps life interesting. Too much stress, however, is not beneficial, but rather harmful and can lead to physical and emotional problems. The number of people who are being treated for stress-related health problems continues to increase and stress-related illness has become a major health concern.

Stress is not caused by viruses, bacteria, or any other infectious agent. Stress does not result directly from an injury. We create stress ourselves by the lifestyle that we have chosen to lead and by the pressures that we either put upon ourselves or allow to be put upon us. We may not be able to prevent all illnesses or injuries, but we can do much to reduce the stress in our lives that often contributes to our physical and emotional problems.

Conclusion

Pain is a part of life. Without it survival would be practically impossible. Knowing this does not make it hurt any less, however. Modern science and medicine can tell us much about the physical causes of pain and have been able to alleviate much of the pain in our world. Even so, pain is still with us. For one reason or another, there are still people around us who are hurting.

Pain and Suffering in the Bible

Jesus went through all the towns and villages, teaching in their synagogues, preaching the good news of the kingdom and healing every disease and sickness.

Matthew 9:35

Someone unfamiliar with the Bible might think that the Scriptures have little to say in regard to the problem of pain and suffering. However, the Bible is not some academic treatise written by lofty intellectuals. Neither is it merely a collection of moral stories that encourage good behavior. Rather, the Bible is a book written by humans about some very real human problems and needs. Aside from being inspired by the Holy Spirit, the writers of the Bible were quite ordinary people. They had the same emotions, fears, and frustrations that we experience today. They knew what it is like to feel exhaustion, hunger, sadness, joy, sorrow, and pain. Actually, it could be argued that these men were much closer to pain, suffering, and death than we are today.

Centuries ago people had wine and maybe a few herbal preparations for pain relief, but that was about it. Antibiotics, medications, anesthetics, surgical and medical procedures, and even aspirin, all of which we tend to take for granted today, were centuries away. In those days medical care was almost nonexistent, and when available, reserved for those who were wealthy enough to afford it. Even those who could afford it, however, had little help for their problems.

Being ill is never pleasant, even in a warm, clean bed with modern medical care. Just imagine yourself back two thousand years ago in damp, dark room with no bed, no heat, and few, if any, medicines. Truly, the writers of the Bible were familiar with pain and suffering.

The authors of the Old and New Testament used a variety of words and phrases to describe the human plight of pain and suffering. Those of us who cannot use the original languages are at somewhat of a loss in understanding the different shades of meaning used by the writers. However, even a careful study of our English translations can give us an insight into the various terms.[1]

In the Old Testament for example, there are various Hebrew words that emphasize both physical and emotional pain (Jer. 15:18; 51:8; Job 33:19). Other words were used to describe sadness, sorrow, and grief (1 Sam. 2:33). Numerous diseases are also described or mentioned in the Old Testament. Some of these include blindness, lameness, paralysis, leprosy, and others.

It is in the New Testament, however, that we find a more complete and personal discussion of pain, sickness, and disease. The writers of the New Testament used Greek words and phrases to explain, describe, and emphasize pain. One such word is found numerous times and is translated into English words such as "distress," "grief," "sorrow," "pain," and "painful" (John 16:20-22; Rom. 9:12; 2 Cor. 2:1,3,7; 7:10; Phil. 2:27; Heb. 12:11; 1 Peter 2:19). Another word is used to describe the pain associated with childbirth and is used in both a literal and figurative manner (Matt. 24:8; Mark 13:8; 1 Thess. 5:3).

In the King James Version the word" suffer" is often used in the sense of experiencing something or even allowing something to occur (for example, "suffer the little children to come unto me"). There are specific Greek words, however, which do refer to suffering in the sense of physical and emotional pain. In modern versions these words are usually translated in a manner that conveys this meaning (Matt. 16:21; 17:12; Mark 5:26; 8:31; Luke 17:25; 24:26; Acts 17:3; Heb. 13:12).

Finally, there are also Greek words that were used specifically to describe a type of sickness or disease. In the Gospels alone there are dozens of references to sickness, disease, and suffering. There are words for weakness, sickness, and physical suffering (Matt. 4:23; 8:17; 9:35; Mark 1:34; 6:5; John 6:2), sickness caused by demons (Mark 6:13; Luke 8:2; 13:11-12), and lingering illness (Matt. 14:14). There are other references to specific diseases such as leprosy (Matt. 10:8; Luke 7:21-22), blindness, lameness, deafness (Luke 7:21-22; John 5:3), and paralysis (John 5:3).

Other New Testament books have references to diseases such as palsy or paralysis (Acts 8:7; 9:33), being crippled (Acts 3:2), digestive trouble (1 Tim. 5:23), dysentery (Acts 28:8), abdominal worms (Acts 12:21-23), and nervous disorders (Acts 5:16). Also, at least four persons are mentioned having some type of illness: Peter's mother-in-law (Mark 1:29-31), Dorcas (Acts 9:37), Epaphroditus (Phil. 2:26-27), and Trophimus (2 Tim. 4:20).[2]

Conclusion

It can be seen that the writers of the Bible were familiar with pain and suffering. In both the Old and New Testaments various words and expressions were used to describe diseases and other types of physical and emotional problems. Many of the diseases mentioned in the Bible have been identified with ones that are still with us today.

In the Gospels we find more frequent references to disease and diseases. Perhaps this is an indication of the importance of the healing ministry of Jesus. We can also see some of the desire on the part of these people to relieve pain and discomfort. This is evident, for example in the determination of the man who wanted to be healed at the pool of Bethesda (John 5:1-15) and the intense hope of the men as they brought their paralyzed friend to Jesus (Mark 2: 1- 12).

The Problem of Pain

> As he went along, he saw a man blind from birth. His disciples asked him, "Rabbi, who sinned, this man or his parents, that he was blind?"
>
> John 9:1-2

When we ourselves are hurting, when we see the pain and suffering of others, or when we hear of some type of tragedy, we are often left with questions such as: "Why did this happen?" or more personally, "Why did this happen to me?" Often these questions are directed at God. We may, for example, hear people say: "Why did God allow this to happen?" or "Where was God when this happened?"

Left unanswered, such questions can seriously affect a person's faith. J. B. Phillips has pointed out that the "problem of evil" and the "problem of pain" are "the most serious problems which face anyone of intelligence and sensibility." He further points out that when faced with suffering or tragedy, people may ask: "If there is a God of Love. . . how can he allow so much suffering in his creation, how can he permit natural disasters such as earthquakes, and how can we possibly reconcile the existence of evil with the idea of an all-wise, all-powerful, all-loving God?"[1]

What Might Have Been

God could have created a perfect world filled with perfect beings. He could have created an environment in which there is no pain, illness, or even death. We would have been, however, not much more than desensitized robots, incapable of any feeling and programmed to carry out some predetermined existence. He chose rather to create us as conscious beings capable of feeling not only pain, sorrow, and sadness, but also feelings such as joy, happiness, friendship, and love.

Along with these capabilities God gave us responsibilities. He created us with the power of choice. It began in the Garden of Eden and continues to this very day. We direct our own behavior by the choices that we make--to do right or to do wrong.

Much of the pain and suffering in the world is caused by wrong choices. Many people attempt to put the blame on God when it really should be upon themselves. Skeptics have for centuries blamed God for the suffering in this world, and even believers have at times pointed to God as the cause of their problems. The real causes of pain and suffering, however, lie elsewhere.

The cause of much of the pain and suffering in the world can be summarized in one word--sin. The Bible teaches that the consequences of sin are ultimately spiritual, but sin can also cause tremendous physical and emotional suffering as well.

The extent to which sin can result in physical, emotional, and even spiritual suffering can be seen, for example, in alcoholism. Alcoholism is a disease. Long-term abuse of alcohol leads to physical and mental symptoms of disease. Alcoholism is also a sin. As someone once said, alcoholism is a sin that becomes a disease.

Think for a moment of all the problems caused by alcohol--the illness, lost jobs, abused spouses and children, broken homes, and innocent people injured or killed by drunk drivers. All of these are caused by sin. Alcoholism begins with a choice--whether or not take the first drink. The same is true of any other sinful act. The person chooses to engage in sin. Often the consequences of that choice are far greater than anyone could imagine.

DISEASE

"Why did God give me this cold?" someone may ask jokingly. The question, however, lies at the root of the problem of pain, suffering, and illness in the world.

Did God actually create diseases? Does God really make people sick? The Jewish people in Jesus' day knew, or thought that they knew, the answer to these questions. For them, disease and illness were caused by sin. It was as simple as that. The Jewish rabbis had taught for centuries that sickness, especially serious illness or physical disability, resulted from punishment from God. Job's friends illustrate this kind of thinking. We can also see examples of this in other places in the Bible. The disciples, for example, one day asked Jesus regarding a blind man, "Who sinned this man or his parents, that he was born blind?" (John 9:2).

There are still people today who hold this view to some extent. In my study of the Bible, however, I can find no support for the view that disease today is some form of divine judgment. God did in Old Testament use "plagues" or other forms of illness to show his power or as a form of punishment. Usually, the plague or sickness was clearly described as a form of punishment, reasons for the punishment were given, and conditions of repentance and removal of the plague were also explained. The type of illness might have been similar to normal disease, but the situation and God's use of the disease were quite different.

In the Gospels we do not find any example of or reference to God using sickness to punish someone (except for incorrect ideas such as the example given above). In Acts there are two examples of what could be called divine judgment: the deaths of Ananias and Saphira and Herod Agrippa. Again, these were explained as a divine act of judgment, and as such are really not relevant to our discussion of disease.

There are numerous references to different types of illness in the New Testament. None of these, however, support the view that illness is a punishment from God. Under the New Covenant our relationship with God is different than it was under the Old. God no longer acts directly as he once did. Rather, the New Testament indicates that God's judgment will occur at the end of time and will be of a spiritual nature rather than physical.

If diseases are not a direct, divine act of punishment, then where did they come from? Biological and medical research has enabled us to understand a great deal about diseases and illness. Today we know that diseases

When man fell in the garden of Eden, too many other things resulted. There weren't many perfections in the world.

are caused by many factors. Since the 19th century we have known that infectious agents, which are more commonly known as "germs," cause many diseases. Most germs are of two types--bacteria and viruses. Bacteria are microscopic, single-celled organisms that literally live everywhere. Most of them cause us no harm and are in fact a part of the biological world. Some of them, however, are known to cause diseases ranging from an infected wound or sore throat to severe and often fatal diseases such as the plague, pneumonia, tuberculosis, and cholera.)

Unlike bacteria, there are no good guys among the viruses. All viruses cause disease. In order to survive, viruses must infect the cells of their host. Viruses are known to infect not only humans but also animals, plants, and even bacteria. Several human diseases are known to be caused by viruses. These range from colds and flu to deadly diseases such as smallpox and AIDS.

There are other diseases, such as cancer, that we do not fully understand. Even with all of our extensive scientific and medical knowledge, we still do not know the exact cause of cancer. It appears that there is probably not one single cause of all cancers. We do know that cancer can be a terrible, uncontrollable disease. Cancerous cells divide, grow, invade, and destroy.

Scientists have also discovered that a number of diseases, called genetic diseases or disorders, are actually inherited in manner similar to other traits. Cystic fibrosis and Huntington's disease are examples of such genetic diseases. Some of these diseases have been successfully treated, but as of yet there are no cures. The Human Genome Project, an international project to identify all of the human genes, may in time help explain and even possibly lead to cures for some genetic diseases.

Environmental factors have also been associated with certain diseases. Construction workers who were unknowingly exposed to asbestos dust have subsequently developed lung cancer. Tobacco smoking has also been shown to increase the incidence of lung cancer. Alcohol has long been known to cause damage to the liver and other parts of the body. Chemicals, pesticides, heavy metals, like mercury or arsenic, and numerous other environmental factors are known to cause disease or at least increase the potential for disease. Some of these we can avoid such as tobacco or alcohol. There may be other detrimental factors in the environment, however, that we may not be aware of or able to avoid.

It is obvious from this brief discussion that there is no one single cause for disease. In addition to those mentioned, there are other forms of illness for which we know little or nothing of their cause. Of those which we do have some knowledge we can see that they are generally caused by some physical agent--an infectious agent or "germ," a genetic defect, or some environmental factor. In other words, diseases seem to be caused by something from within the natural world, such as a virus, or some process, such as a defective gene or cells that lose their natural controls and becomes cancerous.

Did God create diseases? The answer is yes and no. Yes, God did create the physical world and disease is a part of that world. Did God create disease to punish us? No. I do not believe that he did so directly. Disease, like sin and death, is a part of this world because of the Fall. The earth on which we live is imperfect and cursed as a result of the wrong choices that were made in the Garden of Eden.

Physical Laws of the Universe

Scientists have discovered many physical laws that govern the universe. As Christians we believe that these are a part of God's creation. Science has described many of these laws and given them names such as gravity and thermodynamics. We can use our understanding of these laws to explain the motion of planets or why your soup gets cold.

By manipulating these laws we can make cars go and airplanes fly. Yet these same laws, or others like them, cause people to be injured or lose their lives in car accidents and plane crashes. The laws of nature also cause earthquakes, floods, tornadoes, volcanic eruptions, and other "natural disasters." We know that these are part of the natural world and would probably not think much about them if there were no injuries, loss of life, or destruction of property.

Does God use these laws to punish us? In Old Testament times God did use agents such as these to punish people. "Fire and brimstone," for example, would well describe a volcanic eruption. In the New Testament, however, we can find no indication that God would use natural disasters to punish us today.

Understanding events such as these in terms of natural processes does not remove or eliminate the hurt that comes from injury, loss of life, or destruction of property. It does, however, help us to see them for what they are--a part of the world in which we live.

Man was made perfect – with the gift of choice. When he/she did the wrong thing in the garden, it would result in suffering, & all those listed below.

Conclusion

We can see that there are various causes for pain and suffering in the world. A great deal of suffering is caused by sin. Sexual immorality, greed, and the desire to control others are the cause of much suffering. Terrible things such as war, murder, rape, and abusive relationships are caused by sins such as these. Others such as alcoholism, drug addiction, and sexually transmitted diseases, result from making the wrong choices. Natural disasters and many accidents are caused by physical laws of the universe. Some of these are preventable, but others seem to be a part of life.

Why does God allow these things to happen? Why didn't he create a world without pain and suffering? Maybe he did, originally. I do not know much about the world before there was sin. Maybe there were no diseases, pain, or suffering of any kind. I do know about the world in which we now live. It has been marred by sin, and when sin came into the world, it brought with it pain, suffering, and death.

Job and the Problem of Suffering

Have you considered my servant Job?

Job 1:8

We actually know very little about the book of Job and its characters.[1] We do not know, for example, who wrote the book or when it was written. The characters, Job and his friends, appear from the context to have lived during the time of the Patriarchs and the book itself is perhaps the oldest in the Bible. The Jews accepted the book as a part of their Bible, but even the Jewish scholars knew little of the background of the book. Job is one of the most interesting yet elusive books in the Bible.[2] It is a book that we seldom study but one that can give us better insights into the problem of pain.

The book of Job can be divided into three parts. The first of these is the Introduction or Prologue (chapters 1-2). This section, like the conclusion, was written in prose. In the Introduction the main characters are introduced and the stage is set for the remainder of the book. It is here that we are introduced to Satan ("the Accuser"). In a passage that is unique in Scripture we see Satan speaking with God. We also can understand from the Introduction that it is Satan who is the cause of the terrible destruction and suffering that Job experienced.

The second section of the book was written in poetry. This includes chapter 3 where Job initially speaks out about his situation, chapters 4-37 that contain a dialogue between Job and his friends, and finally God's response to Job (38:1-42:6).

The third section is the Conclusion (42:7-17). Here we read of Job's healing and the blessings that he received from God in his later life.

JOB AND THE PROBLEM OF PAIN AND SUFFERING

Job, the main character of the book, is described as a morally upright, deeply religious man with a large family and considerable wealth. Through a series of catastrophes Job suffers the loss of most of his family, his wealth, and finally his own health. Sitting in the dust covered with painful sores, Job asks the universal question: "Why is this happening to me?"

Job's losses were devastating, but so was the response of his friends to his plight. It was common in Bible times for people to interpret illness, loss of relatives, loss of status or finances, and other types of suffering to be the result of sin. In other words it was thought that the person was being punished by God for some type of disobedience. Thus, the conclusion of Job's friends was simple. Basically, they said to him, "Job, you are being punished; therefore you must have sinned. Repent and God will heal you."

Job, however, steadfastly replied, "No. I did not sin and I am innocent. I do not deserve to be punished and cannot understand why God is doing this to me."

Job's losses were physical--his family, his wealth, and finally his own health. Job also faced problems that were spiritual. You see, like his friends, Job also believed that God blesses those who serve him and punishes those who disobey him. Thus, Job faced what he himself perceived to be undeserved punishment. Struggling to understand his situation, Job asked, "Why is God punishing me?"

Suffering from feelings of helplessness and despair, Job cursed the day of his birth and longed for death to release him (3:1-10, 13-19; 6:8-13). For Job anything, even death, seemed better than the pain that he was experiencing. He was angry, despondent, depressed, and felt that life was not worth living.

It will help us to understand Job's feelings when we realize that he was suffering from grief. Grief is an emotional process that a person experiences as the result of some sort of severe trauma or loss. One of the most important studies of grief was done by a psychiatrist named Elizabeth Kubler-Ross.[3] Initially this study was based on interviews with terminally ill patients and later the study was expanded to include those suffering from other types of grief as well.

Based on the findings of the study, Kubler-Ross concluded that grief is not a single emotion, but rather involves several types of emotions. She also found that grief tends to follow a pattern, which has come to be known as the stages of grief. Theses stages are:denial, anger, bargaining, depression, and acceptance. Kubler-Ross described grief is an ongoing process and recognized that a person must work through these stages going from one to another before healing can take place.[4]

Job is obviously suffering from grief over his losses. Throughout the book Job expresses various stages of grief such as anger, bargaining, and depression. Realizing this helps us to understand Job and his situation. Understanding grief will also help us as we experience pain and loss in our own lives.

GOD SPEAKS TO JOB

Following the dialogue between Job and his friends we find a section in the book in which God speaks directly to Job (38:1-42:6). We might initially expect God to answer Job's questions, but such is not the case. In fact, on first impression, these speeches seem out of place in the book.

God did not provide an explanation for pain and suffering in the world, or even for Job's situation for that matter. Instead, God described various aspects of the physical and biological world. These are very majestic and speak of God's greatness and power, but have little to do with Job's dilemma.

Why did God speak to Job in this manner? We really do not know. One author suggested that God's "purpose was not to give Job lessons in cosmology and natural history, and certainly not to browbeat Job with dazzling displays of his power and intelligence (which Job has never for a minute doubted), but to invite Job to reconsider the mystery and complexity and often sheer unfathomableness of the world that God has created."[5]

Only God himself knows the exact reason for responding to Job in this manner. Perhaps the message is that God is in control, even in a world filled with suffering. It also seems to imply that it is unlikely that we will ever fully understand, at least in this present life, why things are this way.

SOME THINGS TO REMEMBER WHEN READING JOB

The study of Job can give us some insights into pain and suffering. When we read the book of Job, however, there are some things that we need to remember. First, we need to remember that God inspired the person who actually wrote the book of Job. It is unlikely, however, that the characters in the book, Job and his friends, were inspired as well. Rather, they were speaking from their own human intelligence, experience, and beliefs. We can identify with Job in many ways, especially when we ourselves are hurting. We can also learn from Job and the others in the book, but they are not the last word on suffering.

Secondly, we need to remember that God's revelation was progressive. More information was often revealed as time progressed. Because of this, therefore, concepts related to pain, suffering, and death found in the book of Job, may not be as complete as those revealed later in the New Testament. It is only in God's completed revelation, especially in the person of Jesus and in his ministry of healing and his resurrection from the dead, that we can ever hope to find understanding for the pain, suffering, and death that we see in our world.

Third, we need to remember that it was common in Bible times for people to interpret illnesses or loss, as punishment for sin. This was the basic belief of Job and his friends, and any statements made by them and recorded in the book of Job reflect this viewpoint. Thus, we need to use caution in drawing conclusions or applying statements made by Job or his friends to our situation today.

Conclusion

In the book of Job we find a man that is hurting and most of us can readily identify with him in his pain. Job is also struggling with his faith and in times of sorrow and grief, we may also identify with him in this as well.

The book of Job reminds us that we live in a world that is marred by sin. God had created an existence for mankind that was perfect and free of pain and suffering, but that was all changed by the Fall. God allows suffering to exist, but he is not the cause of it. Neither does God use pain or suffering as a form of punishment, as Job and his friends incorrectly assumed.

Perhaps the main point of the book of Job is that it is Satan and the evil that he brings in the world is the primary cause of pain and suffering that we see around us.

Suffering and God's Providence

He had James, the brother of John, put to death with the sword.

Acts 12:2

I remember an incident that took place in a Bible class several years ago. The lesson was from Acts 12, and the teacher described how wonderful it was that God had rescued Peter from prison. He went on to say that this shows us how God acts on behalf of his people and that he will in a similar way guide and protect us if we obey him. I raised my hand and said, "We can see from this that God rescued Peter from prison, but in this same chapter we see that James was also put in prison and then beheaded. Does this mean that God saved Peter's life, but allowed James to die?"

I am afraid that my question upset the teacher, probably because he did not have an answer. Or, if he did have an answer, it was not one that he really wanted to face.

He was perfectly willing to have God acting in a manner that would spare Peter's life, but unwilling to allow God to have any part in the death of James. This is how we usually tend to look at providence. When good and positive things happen in our lives, we think that God is acting providentially in our behalf. However, when difficulties and problems arise, we tend to think that God has forgotten about us or even that he is punishing us for something that we have done.

I think that this story illustrates a common problem. It is very difficult for us to understand the nature of God and how he acts in the physical world. We as humans are finite creatures and are limited in many ways by our finiteness. As an infinite being, however, God does not have such limitations. God, for example, is not limited by space or time. He can essentially be everywhere at the same time. He can exist in the present and look not only back into the past, but he can also, if he wants to, look centuries into the future. Because God is not limited by space and time, he can also look at something from "every angle." In other words, God can see not only a particular situation but also everything related to that situation. Thus, a situation that to us appears to be "bad," may ultimately turn out to be something positive. However, only God with his broad perspective and infinite wisdom could foresee this.

The word "providence" is usually used in reference to some act of God on behalf of a person or persons. The case of Peter's release from prison is one such example. In attempting to understand this event, we must first recognize that it was a miracle. Miracles can be thought of as events that interrupt or alter the course of natural events. Jesus, in calming the storm or healing a person of blindness, lameness, or some other disease, obviously interrupted or altered the natural process. Jesus, Peter, and Paul are reported to have raised people from the dead. Such events are contrary to nature and thus clearly miraculous. We recognize them as such because the natural course of events was altered or interrupted.

The account of Peter's rescue from prison in Acts 12 was clearly a miracle. God intervened in the situation and altered the outcome of the events. God has intervened miraculously numerous times in history and many of these are recorded in the Bible. There is really no reason to assume that God could not act miraculously today if he wanted to.

There was a time when God empowered certain persons, such as the apostles and others, with the ability to perform miracles. That time has passed, and no one today has this capability. However, that does not mean that God himself could not act miraculously in our world today. At this very moment God may be acting in a miraculous way in the life of some person. We must remember, however, that miracles are rare events. If such things happened frequently and regularly, then they would no longer be miracles.

Many of us have heard of situations that could be attributed to the miraculous. For example, a person walks away from a terrible accident and the authorities are amazed that the person even survived, let alone was unhurt. Or, a case in which the physicians have said that they can do nothing more, and yet the patient recovered.

Some people may feel that such events are merely "luck" or "chance." Personally, I think it would be very difficult to live day in and day out believing that only "blind chance" or "fate" controlled the events in my life. For the believer the release of Peter from prison or the recovery of someone from a serious, seemingly terminal illness points to the hand of God.

As Creator of the universe, God also acts indirectly through natural processes. He has given to humans, for example, the resources and intelligence to develop and utilize things that will protect us, treat diseases, and lengthen and enhance our lives. Medical procedures, antibiotics, and vaccines are just a few examples.

Perhaps we need to return to the initial subject under consideration, that of Peter and James. It seems logical to conclude that Peter was released from prison through the direct, miraculous intervention of God. James, however, was imprisoned and died at the hands of his enemies. Why would God save Peter's life, but allow James to be executed? This is not an easy question to answer. First of all, we do not know the mind of God. We do not know his reasons or motives for acting in a certain way. Also, as pointed out earlier, we are limited by our finiteness. We know and understand only this physical existence in which we now live. We have no concept of what happens at death or of the spiritual realm. Thus, in our limited way we find it difficult to understand God's actions. From our perspective the death of James seems to be defeat. The "bad guys" won again. For James that may not be necessarily true. He went to be with the Lord, and so for him it was victory rather than defeat.

Sometimes bad things do happen to good people. That does not mean that God is not aware of the situation or does not care. If God intervened in each and every situation, then there would be no natural laws governing the universe and human beings would no longer be free agents with the choice of right or wrong.

God is aware of every situation and does care about each individual. Sometimes God may act is a given situation, but not always. Regardless of whether or not God acts in a miraculous way or not, he is still there and still concerned. This seems to be what Paul meant when he wrote:"And we know that in all things God works for the good of those who love him. . ." (Rom. 8:28).

Perhaps this is the best way to understand providence. In everything that happens to us, both good and bad, God is still at work, still in control, and still has our interest in mind. We may not understand why a particular thing happens in our lives, but we know that no matter what happens God is still with us.

Conclusion

In both the Old and New Testaments we can read examples of God's providential care of his people. Does God still care providentially for his people today? Personally, I believe that he does. God may never open a prison door for us or raise a loved one from the dead. However, he might lead us to a certain decision or plan or a particular course of action. God may even act more directly in a person's life. If we do not believe this, then why pray for his guidance, recovery of a person from illness, safety of someone traveling, or make any other request on behalf of others or ourselves?

From our study of the imprisonment of Peter and James, however, we can see that for some reason, known only to him, God may choose to not intervene in a given situation.

We must realize that whatever happens is within the ultimate plan of God. He is not limited as we are by time and space, so he is able to see what we might call the "big picture." Circumstances, which we might now think of as unpleasant, hurtful, or even unfair on God's part, may eventually turn out in a positive way.

The Christian and Suffering

> *Man born of woman is of a few days and full of trouble.*
>
> Job 14:1

In some ways Christians are not much different than others. This is especially true regarding pain and suffering. Christians hurt and see others hurting, and want to know why. There are no easy answers, but being a Christian and understanding the true meaning of our existence may help us at least to come to terms with this problem.

Life Is Not Fair

In attempting to understand this problem, we must realize first of all that life is not fair. I noticed one day a car in the parking lot of the grocery store that had a bumper sticker that read, "Life is hard and then we die." Although extremely pessimistic, this does fairly well describe the world in which we live. There are many "hard things" in life, and often these come to those who deserve them the least.

We have all seen innocent people suffering while the wicked seem to prosper, and this just does not seem right. We are not the first ones to be bothered by this, however. In the Psalms we read these words:

> Surely God is good to Israel, to those who are pure in heart. But as for me, my feet had almost slipped; I had nearly lost my foothold. For I envied the arrogant when I saw the prosperity of the wicked. They have no struggles; their bodies are healthy and strong. They are free from the burdens common to man; they are not plagued by human ills . . . This is what the wicked are like--always carefree, they increase in wealth. Surely in vain have I kept my heart pure; in vain I have washed my hands in innocence. All day long I have been plagued; I have been punished every morning (Psalm 73:1-5,12-14).

Often the Psalms seem to spring forth from the very depths of human existence, and this example is no different. Such words come from the heart of a troubled soul and express so eloquently our own feelings. We look around us and see so much pain and suffering, especially of innocent people. We also see people living in sin, at times in obvious defiance of God, who seem at least to be untouched by such problems.

Doesn't God know about this? Doesn't he realize that good people are suffering while the wicked seem to prosper? Of course he does. Think about the life of Jesus. He never said or did an unkind thing. Everywhere he went he helped people and did good. Yet he was betrayed, mistreated, and finally brutally murdered.

If God knows about these inequities, then why doesn't he put an end to them? Why doesn't God "terminate" evil and wickedness in the world? We noticed earlier that God couldn't do this, at least not without destroying the free will that he gave to mankind. The answer lies, you see, not in this life or in this world, but in the next. The Psalmist continued, "When I tried to understand all this, it was oppressive to me till I entered the sanctuary of God; then I understood their final destiny" (Psalms 73: 16-17).

There are many things in life that are not fair, and some of them may come into our own lives. When this happens we need to know that God is aware of our difficulties, that he is with us, and that someday all will be made right. In that final day all accounts will be balanced, all dues will be reckoned, and every inequity made equal.

God Did Not Promise To Take Away Our Problems

We must also understand that God did not promise to take away our problems. As mentioned earlier, when I was younger, I thought that Christians really should not have any problems in life. I have lived long enough now to realize that I was wrong. The Christian life is a wonderful life, but Christians have problems in their lives just like everyone else. Pain, disease, and hurting of every kind are common to Christians as well as non-Christians.

A great deal of the suffering in this world is caused by sin. The Christian's sins have been forgiven, and with God's help he or she can live a life free of the dominion of sin. A Christian may, however, experience physical or emotional problems from past sins. A Christian who was an alcoholic, for example, will still suffer from the consequences of his or her previous behavior.

Christians are also subject to the limitations of this physical existence. Thus, illness, sadness, loneliness, and death plague the Christian as well as those who claim no allegiance to Christ.

Although some popular evangelists may claim otherwise, there is nothing in the New Testament to suggest that God has promised to take away the problems of the Christian. That is not to say, however, that God has abandoned his people. He has in fact promised to be with us. In a verse that we have already noticed, Paul said, "And we know that in all things God works for the good of those who love him, who have been called according to his purpose" (Romans 8:28). Those words were written by a man who had suffered terribly, not because of any crimes that he had committed but rather because of his faith. Beaten, stoned, shipwrecked, and imprisoned, Paul had suffered for the cause of Christ. Yet he could still say that God is with us in all things. Those who are in Christ can rest in the assurance that God is with us in all things--in good times and bad, in happiness and sadness, in health and sickness, and even in death.

God Is Not Merely A Spectator

A spectator is one who sits in the stands, watching the game. God is not merely a spectator--he is a participant. John wrote, "The Word became flesh and made his dwelling among us" (John 1: 14a). The incarnation, or God in the flesh, is not an easy concept to grasp. For centuries scholars and theologians have tried to explain this mystery. It is difficult enough for us to understand that we ourselves have both physical and spiritual elements that make up our being. Jesus Christ, on the other hand, was totally God and yet totally human. He was at the same time a part of the godhead and also a human being. During his earthly existence God, in the form of Jesus the Son, clothed himself in the flesh of humanity. He retained the power and authority of the Son of God but at the same time experienced the feelings of a man. He was not a spectator but a participant.

This was especially true in the crucifixion of Jesus. Isaiah described it in these words:

> He was despised and rejected by men, a man of sorrows, and familiar with suffering. Like one from whom men hide their faces he was despised, and we esteemed him not. Surely he took up our infirmities and carried our sorrows, yet we considered him stricken by God, smitten by him, and afflicted. But he was pierced for our transgressions, he was crushed for our iniquities; the punishment that brought us peace was upon him, and by his wounds we are healed. We all, like sheep, have gone astray, each of us has turned to his own way; and the Lord has laid on him the iniquity of us all. He was oppressed and afflicted, yet he did not open his mouth; he was led like a lamb to the slaughter, and as a sheep before her shearers is silent, so he did not open his mouth. By oppression and judgment he was taken away. And who can speak of his descendants? For he was cut off from the land of the living; for the transgression of my people he was stricken (Isaiah 53: 4-8).

Although written centuries before the actual event, this is perhaps the most graphic description of the crucifixion in all of Scripture. Notice the words, especially the verbs: "despised," "rejected," "pierced," "crushed," "oppressed," and "afflicted." These are powerful words used to describe someone who has suffered intensely.

When we hurt, we need to remember that God, the Creator of the universe, understands. Jesus, his Son, has experienced feelings and emotions as we have. When we pray, we do not pray to some distant and unknowing being. Rather, we pray to one who has known physical and emotional pain and has experienced even death.

Nothing In This Life Is Permanent

As human beings in this physical world our understanding is very limited. Everything we feel, understand, and for the most part value, is in this world. We know little of the spiritual world and even less about eternity.

Our bodies, however, were not meant to last forever. Neither was this physical universe. Like our bodies, the universe is also slowly running down and wearing out. There must be something beyond this physical existence. If not, then life is not worth very much.

Christians need to realize that nothing in this life is permanent. We live in this world, but we are not of this world. Those who are in Christ have been redeemed, sanctified, and prepared for an eternal existence, but not in this world. When a person realizes that sixty, seventy, even eighty or more years of life are nothing compared to eternity, then he or she can begin to put things into proper perspective.

There is nothing wrong with loving or enjoying life to

its fullest as long as a person has the right priorities. Jesus himself no doubt enjoyed life. He had friends, laughed, and enjoyed himself. But when it came time to die, he was ready even though he knew it was not going to be easy.

It is hard to give up friends and loved ones and may be more difficult to give up life itself. But if we have the right attitude and priorities and are in the right relationship with God, then we have nothing to worry about.

Conclusion

G. K. Chesterton once used the analogy of the "wrong side of the tapestry" in one of his stories. The figure of the tapestry is also quite fitting to this discussion. When you stand before a tapestry, you see a beautiful picture woven in colored threads. On the other side, the "wrong side" of the tapestry, however, there is only knotted and uneven strands of thread. The image of the tapestry is difficult or even impossible to see from this side. Such is our understanding of human existence--we can see only one side of the tapestry, and it is the wrong side. We can only partially make out the image of eternal existence, and what we can see is very limited. It is at this point that faith must take over. We need to have what J. B. Phillips described as "the attitude of mind which is rooted in eternity." It is only when we realize that our physical existence is temporary and only a part of the whole, and that our understanding of the true meaning of life is incomplete, that we can begin to come to grips with sin, pain, suffering, and death in the world around us.

Death: the Final Enemy

The last enemy to be destroyed is death.

1 Corinthians 15:26

I still remember my first encounter with death, at least the first time that I understood what was happening. My brother and I were in elementary school. One day we were called to the office and when we arrived there I knew something was seriously wrong because my dad was there. He worked in a factory and was very seldom at home during the day. When we were outside he explained that our grandmother had died. Although that was many years ago, I still remember the sick feeling in the pit of my stomach--a mixture of hurt, fear, and helplessness. As an adult I may understand more about life and death, but I still have some of those same feelings about death that I had as a child.

Death as an Enemy

Mankind has truly subdued the earth. We have conquered both land and sea and have traveled to the moon. We have eliminated many diseases through the development of antibiotics and vaccines. We have lengthened the lives of many people through surgical and medical techniques. We have not, however, been able to conquer death.

Death has always been viewed as the enemy, and many have sought in vain to subdue this adversary. The alchemists of the Middle Ages sought not only a means to change lead into gold but also a source of immortality--the "elixir of life." Many of the explorers who came to the New World sought not only riches but also that same elusive prize, the ability to live forever--the fabled "fountain of youth."

Today, some try to prolong their lives by special diets or exotic treatments, but they too will eventually die. Death is, in a way, an inevitable part of living. It is, however, an unwanted guest. It comes into our lives, and there is little that we can do about it. Death is the enemy.

For many death is the ultimate disaster--it is annihilation or extinction. It is the end or termination of life or existence. We speak, for example, of a "terminal illness," which conveys the idea of the end or cessation of something. To some it is the end of physical life, but to others it is the obliteration of existence.

Death is never easy to accept. But must we view death as the ultimate disaster? Is death really termination or extinction of existence? The answer to these questions is emphatically NO. The grim, hopeless view of death held by many is in stark contrast to the vision of death that should be held by those who are in Christ.

Christians are not left groping in darkness and ignorance of the unknown. Death is dealt with quite openly and frankly in the Bible. The message of the Bible is clear--it is a message of hope. The empty tomb and the resurrected Lord are the ties that bind us to the hope that we have as Christians.

DEATH AS A SYMBOL

It is perhaps ironic, but certainly fitting that baptism, the manner in which we enter into the body of Christ, or the church, is itself a symbol of death. Paul said in regard to our baptism: "Or do you not know that all of us who were baptized into Christ were baptized into his death? We were therefore buried with him through baptism into death in order that, just as Christ was raised from the dead through the glory of the Father, we too may live a new life. If we have been united with him in his death, we will certainly also be united with him in his resurrection" (Rom. 6:3-5).

Thus, the symbolic death and burial of baptism unites us with his death, and arising from the watery grave unites us symbolically with the resurrection of our Lord, Jesus Christ.

Baptism is also symbolic of the death of the body of sin. Again, Paul wrote:"For we know that our old self was crucified with him so that the body of sin might be rendered powerless, that we should no longer be slaves to sin--because anyone who has died has been freed from sin" (Rom. 6:6-7).

A missionary once told the story of a man who was baptized. After the baptism he had dressed and was about to leave when the missionary noticed that he had forgotten his coat. He said to the man, "You have forgotten your coat." The new Christian replied, "No I haven't. I have a new coat for I have put on Christ. That old coat is my old life which I now leave behind." Although this man may have had a limited knowledge of God and the Bible, he had a very accurate picture of baptism and the death that it symbolizes. It takes someone like this man, who had to make drastic changes in his life to become a Christian, to fully understand the "death" which occurs in baptism.

Death Is Not Final

For someone living outside of Christ there is little hope in death. For them death is the end. As biological life departs from the body, that person ceases to exist. The physical remains are placed into the earth, and decay will return the body to the chemical elements of which it was composed. Death is final.

Such hopelessness is indescribable. Personally, I cannot fully understand or even grasp such a perspective of life and death. Fortunately, there is no need to do so. In John 11: 25 Jesus said, "I am the resurrection and the life." Death is not final. Death is not the end.

Jesus' words were not merely some hypothetical statement. We are not left without testimony or evidence regarding the resurrection. In the New Testament we can read about five individuals who were raised from the dead. These events were not done in secret but rather were done openly and left no question in the minds of those present. The writers record these events in a matter-of-fact way and leave little doubt that they, as well as those other early Christians, had complete confidence in the validity of the accounts.

In the Gospels we can read the account of Jesus raising three individuals from the dead. These were Jairus' daughter (Matt. 9:18-26), the widow's son at Nain (Luke 7:11-17), and Lazarus (John 11:1-44). Two others were raised from the dead in Acts. Peter raised Tabitha or Dorcas (Acts 9:32-43), and Paul raised the young man Eutychus, who had fallen out of the window and died (Acts 20:7-12).

There could have been others of which we have no record. But the point is that we have ample evidence upon which to base our faith.

One of these occurrences stands out from the others. In my opinion the raising of Lazarus is of greater significance. The other four persons had been dead for only a short time, anywhere from a few minutes to probably not more than a few hours (since burial was typically the same day or the next morning if the person died late in the day). In these cases the injury or disease that had caused the death was repaired, or healed, and life was miraculously restored to the individual. We can perhaps understand this better today with our knowledge of modern medical methods of resuscitation and organ transplants. That is not, however, to decrease the miraculous element or to suggest that we have the same capabilities today with cardiac defibrillators and other medical procedures.

The raising of Lazarus was different. He had been dead four days. Lazarus had died, was placed in the tomb, and the processes of decay had begun to destroy his physical body. Jesus, in raising Lazarus from the dead, did not merely return life to a body as had taken place in the other four cases. Rather, Jesus had to miraculously reverse the processes of decay and place the spirit of Lazarus back into this physical body. This could leave no doubt in anyone's mind that Lazarus had been perhaps unconscious or that some mistake had been made and that he was not actually dead. Death and decay had claimed Lazarus, and only the miraculous power of Jesus could return him to life.

Lazarus and the others were raised from the dead. Their physical lives were returned to them, but only for a few years at the most. Like others before and after them, they eventually died again, and their physical bodies were returned to the dust. Such will it be with us unless the Lord returns during our lifetime.

To be raised from the dead only to die again, although a great miracle, does not give us the assurance that we want and need. For this assurance we must look to another death and another resurrection--that of Jesus.

There is a very beautiful account in the last chapter of Mark. Mary Magdalene, Mary the mother of James, and Salome awoke early in the morning and brought spices to the tomb to anoint the body of Jesus. He had been hastily buried because of the approaching Sabbath, and his body had not been properly prepared for burial. As they walked along, they discussed how they might move the large stone that sealed the tomb. Mark recorded these words:"But when they looked up, they saw that the stone, which was very large, had been rolled away. As they entered the tomb, they saw a young man dressed in a white robe sitting on the right side, and they were alarmed. 'Don't be alarmed,' he said. 'You are looking for Jesus the Nazarene, who was crucified. He is risen! He is not here. See the place where they laid him'" (Mark 16:4-6).

Jesus himself had died and was buried. The lifeless body of the one who had healed so many and had raised his good friend Lazarus from the dead, had been placed in a tomb. These women planned to do the last thing that they could for Jesus, to anoint his body for burial, as was the practice of that time. Little did they expect to find the tomb empty, nor did they anticipate the words of the angel, "He is risen! He is not here."

Jesus had arisen from the dead, but his resurrection was not like the others. In Romans we read these words: "For we know that since Christ was raised from the dead, he cannot die again; death no longer has mastery over him. The death he died, he died to sin once for all; but the life he lives, he lives to God" (Rom. 6:9-10).

Jesus through his resurrection conquered death. Paul states that death no longer has "mastery" or "dominion" or "power" over him. J. B. Phillips translated this passage as follows: "We can be sure that the risen Christ never dies again--death's power to touch him is finished."

The empty tomb and the resurrected Lord are the basis for our hope and assurance that death is not final. We will all lose loved ones to this enemy, and it is certain that unless the Lord returns first, we also will someday die. But if we are in Christ, then we need not dread death, as do those without this hope. As Christians, the power of death cannot touch us for we share not only in the death of Christ but in his resurrection as well.

THE ANALOGY OF THE SEED

For many people death is viewed as the end or cessation of life. For the Christian, however, such is not the case. The Bible teaches us that death is just the means of passing from one existence to another. Although we have the assurance of the Scriptures, even Christians may at times have moments of worry, fear, and even at times doubt. Evidently we are not alone for death is a frequent topic of discussion in the New Testament. It would appear, for example, that the Christians in Corinth had some concerns that were addressed by Paul. Using an analogy of a seed planted in the soil, Paul wrote:"When you sow, you do not plant the body that will be, but just a seed, perhaps of wheat or something else. But God gives it a body as he has determined, and each kind of seed he gives its own body" (1 Cor. 15:37-38).

He goes on to say:"So it will be with the resurrection of the dead. The body that is sown is perishable, it is raised imperishable; it is sown in dishonor, it is raised in glory; it is sown in weakness, it is raised in power; it is sown a natural body, it is raised a spiritual body" (1 Cor. 15:42-44).

I do not know the extent of Paul's knowledge of plants, but I am a biologist, and perhaps for this reason the passage means more to me. Inside of every seed is an embryo, or baby plant. This embryo is, in a sense, confined in the seed; its only hope of escape is to be planted and allowed to germinate. In the soil the seed splits open, the embryo is released from its prison, and a new life begins.

Such is our human existence. We have a part of us, which is immortal, but like the seed, it is housed in our physical body. This prison house of our physical body is plagued by the limitations of time; it is ravaged by disease, infirmity, and old age. The spirit, on the other hand, is immortal and imperishable. Disease, old age, death, and other constraints of this life will have no effect on our spiritual bodies.

In death, the spirit, like the embryo of the seed, is released from its imprisonment. Death, then, allows the spirit to escape from the confines of the physical body. Just as the seed germinates into a new plant, so we shall arise to a new existence in our spiritual body.

The Metaphor Of Sleep

In the New Testament, "sleep" is sometimes used as a metaphor, or figure, for death. In Matthew 9:24 Jesus used the term to describe Jairus' daughter. Perhaps a more well-known passage is in John 11:11 where Jesus said, "Our friend Lazarus has fallen asleep; but I am going there to wake him up."

Probably the most striking usage of the metaphor of sleep for death is in Acts 7:60. Stephen had been brutally murdered by an angry mob. We can only imagine his body, broken and crushed by the stones, lying on the dusty ground. Luke, in recording this incident could have used strong language to denounce this murderous act. He chose rather to write simply "he fell asleep."

Christians have used the metaphor of sleep as a figure describing death ever since this incident early in the history of the church. Commenting on the use of sleep as a metaphor for death, M. R. Vincent has made the following observations:

> Though pagan authors sometimes used sleep to signify death, it was only as a poetic figure. When Christ, on the other hand, said, 'Our friend Lazarus sleepeth,' he used the word not as a figure, but as the expression of a fact. In that mystery of death, in which the pagan saw only nothingness, Jesus saw continued life, rest, waking--the elements which enter into sleep. And thus,

in Christian speech and thought, as the doctrine of the resurrection struck its roots deeper, the word dead with its hopeless finality, gave place to the more gracious and hopeful word sleep. The Pagan burying place carried in its name no suggestion of hope or comfort. It was a burying-place, a hiding-place, a monumentum, a mere memorial of something gone . . . but the Christian thought of death as sleep, brought with it into Christian speech the kindred thought of a chamber of rest, and embodied it in the word cemetery--the place to lie down to sleep.[1]

Conclusion

Many people view death as the ultimate enemy that brings the final end to existence. For Christians, however, such is not the case. Death is still an enemy, but it is an enemy that has been conquered.

Just imagine for a moment what it must have been like when those early disciples traveled through the countryside and first spread the news that even in death there is life. The Good News is that Jesus came to the earth, lived as a human being, died as we will someday die; but, as the angel said to the women early that morning, "He is risen! He is not here."

Those early Christians were willing to suffer persecution and even death for what they believed. Why? Because they had seen the risen Lord and were convinced that death was not the end--only the beginning. As Paul wrote, "Death is swallowed up in victory. For where now, O death, is your power to hurt us? Where now O grave, is the victory you hoped to win?" (1 Cor. 15:54-55 Phillips).

The Christian and Hope

But hope that is seen is no hope at all. Who hopes for what he already has?

Romans 8:24b

"Hope" is an interesting word. In everyday language we use it in all sorts of ways. You might hear someone say, for example, "I hope you have a good day," or "I hope it doesn't rain today," or "I hope our team wins the game tonight." In such cases the word "hope" is used to describe a desire or wish on the part of someone.

The word "hope" when used in the Bible is more than just "wishful thinking." In both the Old and New Testaments the words translated as "hope" carry with them the idea of anticipation and confident expectation.[1] Expectation and anticipation are quite different from merely wishing for something to happen.

Perhaps an analogy will help. When we step into a room we reach for the light switch. Even if the electricity is temporarily off due to a storm, we will flip the switch. It is a habit that is "automatic" with us. Why is that? It is because nearly every other time that we have done so, the lights came on. Only rarely, when the electricity is off or when the bulb has burned out, have we been disappointed. In other words we "expect" or "anticipate" that the lights will come on and that expectation is based on previous experience. "Hope" in the biblical sense is like that. There is confidence, anticipation, and expectation in the hope of the Christian.

Where Is This Hope?

There is only one place to find this hope and that is in Christ. Paul pointed out that all spiritual blessings, including hope, are to be found only in Christ (Eph. 1:3). The phrase "in Christ" is found several times in the New Testament and is always used in reference to being a Christian. In other words, to be in Christ is to be in the right relationship with God. Thus, only those who have been born again through baptism have this hope.

When a person becomes a Christian, there is a great change in that person's life. I remember talking to a young man who described this change in his life. He said, "I knew what I had to do. I had to give up my friends, my drinking buddies, my activities, and the women that I ran around with. Before I became a Christian I would have a few beers when I met a friend, but now we have a cup of coffee."

Many Christians grew up in the church and really never lived a very sinful life. Sometimes it is difficult for such individuals to fully grasp the change that baptism can have on a person's life. This young man, however, did understand the meaning of repentance and the change, which Christianity brought into his life.

We noticed earlier that baptism is a symbolic death. In baptism the old person dies, and a new person comes up out of the water. Not only are all of the new Christian's sins forgiven, but he or she will also have a new outlook on life. Baptism, which puts one into Christ, results in a transformation from helplessness and fear to anticipation, expectation, and hope.

Becoming a Christian may not change a person's situation in life. A person with terminal cancer before baptism, for example, will still have cancer after baptism. The attitude and outlook of that person, however, will be drastically changed. Disease, even death itself, will no longer have the power over that person that it once had. For those who are in Christ, death is not the victor. It still hurts to lose a loved one, and there is still some fear of the unknown, but death no longer has the power that it once had over us.

As we walk from the grave of a loved one, death seems to be so powerful and so final. Where is this hope? Where is this confidence? We noticed earlier that it is in the empty tomb of our Lord. As those women made their way to the tomb that morning, little did they anticipate the events that unfolded before them. The hope, which we have, can be summed up in the words of the angel, "He is risen! He is not here."

THE PROMISE OF BETTER THINGS

All around us we see a world filled with sin, crime, pain, disease, and death. One might even in anger and frustration be tempted to say, "What hope?" We will never find the complete answer to this question in this life. True hope is only to be found in the next life.

We have already seen that the power of death was taken away by the resurrection of Christ and that as Christians we will share in that resurrection. I do not fully understand what it will be like to be resurrected from the dead or to live in heaven for eternity. One day, when our daughter was about seven or eight years old, she said, "What will it be like in heaven?" I must admit that I was somewhat at a loss to answer her question. As I recall, I said something like, "It will be great."

I do know that there will not be any type of sickness or disease in heaven. Neither will there be any loneliness, sadness, pain, sorrow, or other hurtful things. Even if heaven was just like the earth, but all these sorts of things were taken away, it would be a great place.

Heaven, however, is so much more. Jesus is there and he has prepared a place for those who follow him (John 14:3). As Christians, we also have the assurance that Jesus will return and take both the dead and living believers to be with him in heaven (1 Thess. 4:13-18; 2 Cor. 5:1-10). Heaven is also described as a "better country" (Heb. 11:16) and a place of safety (2 Tim. 4:18). Jesus also told us that our reward would be in heaven (Matt. 5:12).

The most complete picture of heaven in the Bible is found in the book of Revelation (Rev. 21:1-22:5). Revelation is a book that was written in what is called apocalyptic language. It is highly figurative and symbolic and often difficult to understand. Even so, this passage can give us a view of heaven that is filled with hope.

First of all, we read here that there will be no more pain, suffering, or death in heaven (21:4). These are a part of the old, physical world in which we now live. None of these will be in the new spiritual existence that we will experience there.

Secondly, we can see from this passage that heaven is really beyond description (21:9-21). The gold, pearls, and precious stones were the most valuable things that were known at the time. These were used to describe heaven, even though heaven is not a physical place where things like this would be found. It seems as though John was searching for some way to describe heaven, but the best that he could do was to use a physical description. And so, he filled that description with the most valuable and beautiful things that he could imagine.

Third, this passage indicates that heaven is a place of security. It is described as a city with walls surrounding it (21:12). At that time a walled city was a sign of wealth and power. It was a secure city that could be defended against its enemies.

Fourth, the description here tells us that heaven is a place of blessings. The flowing river and the abundant crops and fruit, for example, denote blessings from God (22:22). This would have been especially evident to those living in an arid land like the Middle East.

Fifth, we can read that heaven is a place where there is no night (22:5). Freedom from darkness is a great blessing. Darkness is associated with evil, but all that is evil has been excluded from heaven. Darkness is also a time of fear and anxiety. This is especially true for someone who is ill or in pain. But, none of these things are there either.

Deep down within us, we all have a longing for a place just like this. A place of security that is free of the ills of our sin-scarred world, where we can rest and be free from pain and suffering, and where war, poverty, disease, and evil cannot exist. We also long place for a where we can rejoin our loved ones and be with God. There is only one place like that--heaven.

Conclusion

In *The Chronicles of Narnia* by C. S. Lewis, Caspain, the aged and beloved king, is laid to rest. In a very beautiful and fitting figure of Christ, the blood of the great lion, Aslan, is used to revive him and raise him from the dead. His tired, worn, and frail body is transformed again into that of a young prince.

I realize that this is merely a fictional story. But somehow, I think that our resurrection will be something like that. We will exchange our old body for a new one, which is free of aches and pains and other limitations of our physical existence. And in this new body we will live with God, Jesus, the Spirit, and all of God's faithful for ever and ever.

Final Thoughts

When I was growing up a teenage girl in our congregation was killed in a car accident. The following Sunday morning a young man went to the front of the auditorium to lead the closing prayer. He began, stopped, and then after a moment turned and walked out of the building. As far as I know he never came back. When someone went to talk with him he told the person that he could not believe in a God that would allow such a tragic accident to occur.

The realization that there is so much pain in our world can lead a person in one of two directions. Some individuals, like this young man, turn their backs on God. Others look at the world of pain and suffering and turn toward God, believing that the only hope that anyone can have is found in God and his promise of eternal life.

For me personally, it is much more reasonable to believe that there is something beyond this world. If not, then life would be just too meaningless. Pain, suffering, and death would be too unbearable. Life would not be worth living.

It is only by looking at this life in terms of eternity that we can make any sense out of the world in which we live. Elisabeth Elliot wrote: "Think of the shock the crowds must have felt when Jesus said that those who mourn, those who are poor and persecuted and have nothing are *happy!* How could he say such things? Only in light of another kingdom, another world, another way of seeing this world. He came to bring life--another kind of life altogether. And it is in terms of that life that we must learn to look at our sufferings."[1]

Paul put it this way: "In my opinion whatever we may have to go through now is less than nothing compared with the magnificent future God has planned for us" (Rom. 8:18 Phillips). AMEN!

There is so much more waiting for those who are in Christ. Like me, I hope that you too are looking forward to that day. There we will live in a new body and a new place where we will no longer be troubled with the problem of pain and suffering.

Notes

WHAT IS PAIN?
1. Dr. Paul Brand and Philip Yancey, *Pain: The Gift Nobody Wants* (New York: Harper Collins, 1993).
2. Albert Schweitzer, *The Primeval Forest* (Baltimore: Johns Hopkins University Press, 1931), 74.

PAIN AND SUFFERING IN THE BIBLE
1. Helpful references include *The Expository Dictionary of Bible Words* by Lawrence O. Richards (Grand Rapids: Zondervan, 1985) and *An Expository Dictionary of New Testament Words* by W. E. Vine (Old Tappan, NJ: Fleming H. Revell Company, 1940).
2. For a more complete discussion of this topic see Paul E. Adolph, "Diseases," *The New International Dictionary of the Bible*, J. D. Douglas and Merrill C. Tenney eds. (Grand Rapids:Zondervan, 1987), 273-278; and Roland K. Harrison, "Disease" in *International Standard*

Bible Encyclopedia, Geoffrey W. Bromiley, ed. , 4 vols. (Grand Rapids:Eerdmans, 1979), 1:953-960.

THE PROBLEM OF PAIN

1. J. B. Phillips, *God Our Contemporary* (New York:Macmillan, 1960), 87.

JOB AND THE PROBLEM OF SUFFERING

1. For an introduction to the book of Job see *A Survey of Old Testament Introduction* by Gleason L. Archer, Jr. (Chicago: Moody Press, 1964), 438-449.
2. For a different perspective on Job try reading the book in *The Message: The Bible in Contemporary Language* by Eugene H. Peterson (Colorado Springs: NavPress, 2002).
3. Elisabeth Kubler-Ross, *On Death and Dying* (New York: Collier Books, 1969).
4. A helpful book for understanding grief is *Growing Through Grief* by Bill Flatt (Nashville:Christian Communications, 1987).
5. David J. A. Clines, "Job," *The New International Bible Commentary*, F. F. Bruce, ed. (Grand Rapids:Zondervan, 1986), 545.

DEATH: THE FINAL ENEMY

1. M. R. Vincent, *Word Studies in the New Testament* (Grand Rapids: Wm. B. Eerdmans, 1946), 486.

The Christian and Hope

1. Lawrence O. Richards, *The Expository Dictionary Of Bible Words* (Grand Rapids: Zondervan, 1985), 343-345.

Final Thoughts

1. Elisabeth Elliot, *A Path Through Suffering* (Ventura, CA:Regal Books,1990), 25.

Further Reading

Becton, Randy. *Does God Care When We Suffer?And Will He Do Anything About It?* Grand Rapids:Baker, 1988.

Brand, Paul and Philip Yancey. *Pain:The Gift Nobody Wants.* New York: HarperCollins, 1993.

Lewis, C. S. *A Grief Observed.* New York:Seabury Press, 1961.

Lewis, C. S. *The Problem of Pain.* New York:Macmillan, 1962.

Yancey, Philip. *Disappointment with God:Three Questions No One Asks Aloud.* New York:HarperCollins, 1988.

Yancey, Philip. *Where is God When It Hurts?* Grand Rapids:Zondervan, 1990.

CPSIA information can be obtained at www.ICGtesting.com
Printed in the USA
LVOW080747141012

302767LV00001B/151/P